In Whom the Father Delights

M. Basilea Schlink

Lakeland
Marshall Pickering
3 Beggarwood Lane, Basingstoke, Hants RG23 7LP, UK

British Library Cataloguing in Publication Data

Schlink, Basilea
   In whom the Father delights: growing closer
   to God through suffering.
   1. Christian life   2. Faith
   I. Title   II. Wen Gott liebst. *English*
   248.4   BV4509.5

   ISBN 0-551-01169-6

Printed in Great Britain by J. W. Arrowsmith Ltd, Bristol

Contents

"...to do you good in the end"

Stretching far into the distance is a vast multitude
of people — innumerable families with their young
and old trekking through the desert. On they tread
amid untold hardships and in constant peril of
death. Their hearts are heavy, for they have left behind them a land where despite all the toil and op-
pression they were at least provided with the bare
necessities of life.

Now they do not know from one day to the next
where they are to find food for themselves, their little ones and old people in this wilderness. They are
doomed to die. There are no houses to shield them
from the blistering desert sun. Day after day, under
the merciless glare of the sun, they have to cover
long distances with no fixed destination. All they
possess is a dim hope of reaching an unknown
promised land, but — as they well know — unless
miracle upon miracle happens they will die on the
way. Threatened by wild beasts, threatened by
marauding tribes, threatened by over-exposure to
the sun, threatened by starvation — this is their
situation.

A company of sorely-tried and chastened people
trekking through the desert! Who is it that leads
them along such an unspeakably difficult path
where death confronts them with every new day?
Moses tells them that it is the Lord God who is leading them through the wilderness. And this is the
God they are supposed to love? Unable to understand God and His dealings, the people murmur
and complain; they rebel against Him.

Difficult leadings, desert roads, paths of chastening — who of us understands God at such times? The heart cries out, "Why are You leading me *this* way? It's almost breaking me!" A marriage on the rocks, perhaps. Endless troubles with the children. Great loneliness. Severe illness and disablement. Deep disappointments. Or emotional stress. We are all familiar with desert roads where we have given up hope of receiving help. And yet all is not lost. Like a star in the dark night-sky, a bright light shines upon the sorely-tried people of God long ago on their difficult path through the desert. The meaning of this dark path is illuminated for them. God tells them of an "afterwards", a joyful ending to paths of chastening.

God says that He is disciplining in order "to do you good in the end" (Deuteronomy 8:16). Ways of suffering and chastening will not remain as such. Suffering will not be the final outcome. The dark path will end in radiant light. What a message for the people of God in their deep distress and inner conflict! And down through the ages this has been the experience of all who believed in God's promise that dark paths of suffering are followed by an "afterwards" when the heart rejoices and gives thanks for the outcome of suffering. As our Father, God promises us an "afterwards" when He will "do us good in the end". Because His heart overflows with love for us, He cannot lead us into suffering and chastening without letting us experience consolation and happiness in the end. Hard pathways can never end in suffering alone. Of God the Father it is written, "In all their affliction he was afflicted" (Isaiah 63:9). And so His fatherly heart cannot bear to see us experience nothing but suffering.

Indeed, God sacrificed His dearest and best, His only begotten Son, in order to deliver us from all our sins and everything else that makes us unhappy. He rejoices in doing us good (cf. Jeremiah 32:41). He delights in showing mercy, not in executing judgment (cf. Micah 7:18b). It is hard for Him to chasten us. God the Father loves us just as He loved His people, of whom it is said, "The men of Judah are the plant he cherished" (Isaiah 5:7 NEB). This love constrains God to show goodness to His own. Yes, God has lost His heart to sinful human beings like you and me. So dearly does He love us. This is why He always has a wonderful outcome planned for our suffering. This is why He wants to shower us with goodness after we have had to go through a time of suffering and chastening.

However, in order to experience the goodness of God, the gracious outcome He has prepared, we must expect it. This is the precondition. For if we expect the opposite — namely, that our suffering will never come to an end or that it will lead to something terrible — we are not capable of receiving the blessing that awaits us. Our heart is filled with cares, grumbling, complaints and accusations against God. It has no room left for all the love and goodness God wants to show us. This is illustrated in the story of the men who returned from searching out the Promised Land. Those Israelites who only complained, not seeing that the men had much to relate and show that was good, really did perish in the wilderness, overwhelmed by suffering. It was just as they had predicted in their mistrust. How-

ever, Joshua and Caleb, who trusted in God and in
His love, expecting that He would give them something good, received it. They later entered the land
of Canaan amid great rejoicing. And so in times of
suffering the important thing is to believe and expect that the love of God has good things in store
for us. Then we shall experience His goodness.
Otherwise, our suffering will end in misery.

Someone is particularly keen on seeing us driven
to despair by our suffering — and that is Satan, our
mortal enemy. He sows the seeds of mistrust in our
hearts, so that we neither expect God's goodness
nor experience it, reaping unhappiness instead. He
does all he can, so that we do not really accept chastening and suffering but rebel against them, even if
unconsciously. As the fallen Lucifer, he begrudges
us the glory at the throne of God — the glory that he
lost and that is to be ours by virtue of Jesus' redemption. On paths of suffering and chastening we
shall be prepared to receive this glory. Satan also
does his best to make us forfeit the blessing the
Lord has in store for us in this life after we have
completed a path of chastening. He uses disappointments, suffering and the like to get at us. In
the case of Jesus he chose the torment of hunger, as
we read in the story of the Temptation, but he
failed in his bid for victory.

If we are in suffering or having trouble, we can
be sure that Satan is on the scene, prowling around
like a roaring lion seeking whom he may devour
(cf. 1 Peter 5:8). And so when we go through times
of suffering and chastening it is vital that we be on
the alert, cautious as to which voice we heed and
believe. Do we give ear to the Enemy as he tries to

persuade us: "That's just asking too much of you. Your life will be ruined. It's too hard for you. Why you, always you?" Or do we listen to the voice of God speaking to us: "It is I, your Father, who am chastening you, because I love you, My child. Trust Me, I will not let you be tempted beyond your strength. My plans for you are wonderful. My path of chastening will end in happiness, blessing, joy and glory."

Our experience in chastening and suffering depends on which voice we allow into our hearts. Either we shall fall into despair, unable to cope with chastening, and so fail to experience its wonderful outcome; or else we shall be consoled, strengthened and transformed amid chastening and experience a glorious and joyful "afterwards" and abundant blessings.

Just how much the Enemy struggles to gain control over us on paths of chastening, I came to discover especially during one stage in the commission of our Sisterhood many years ago. The Lord's hand was heavy upon us. More buildings were required to accommodate retreat guests, the sick, co-workers, and our growing family of Sisters — but where to build? We needed to acquire the land adjoining the Mother House in order to carry on the ministry entrusted to us. God gave us the inner assurance and a Scripture verse, a word of promise, for this project. And we made it an earnest matter of prayer, firmly believing that God had the power to open the closed gates to this piece of land, which we called "Canaan". But for years the gates remained closed. Whenever a flicker of hope appeared, it was snuffed out again. One impossibility after the other arose; one barrier after the other blocked our way.

For years on end we received nothing but No's from the landowners and the authorities. To make matters worse, we had no money to pay for the land even if we were granted permission to acquire it. In spite of our many and fervent prayers that the treasury would be filled, the windows of heaven remained closed. And so it was impossible to obtain the land, let alone erect the planned buildings.

My daily bread consisted of numerous difficulties, dashed hopes, frustrated plans, disappointments, problems created by those who energetically withstood our attempts to acquire the land, and many tears shed in private. These were chastenings in the truest sense of the word.

Now the time was ripe for the Tempter. Taking advantage of this plight, he sought an inroad into my heart to rob me of the promise I had received from the Lord. "Give up!" his voice said. "Don't go on believing. This project isn't God's will, for He hasn't answered your prayers. That shows that He doesn't want to help this time. Stop following this path, which brings you nothing but disappointments, struggles, suffering and unnecessary work. It will only end in a fiasco!" Then came the warnings or even derision of others, who declared that we would never be able to carry out our project. Time and again the voice of the Evil One nagged at me, "Don't keep on praying. Give up the struggle. This project is not God's will; otherwise He would have answered your prayers!"

But then came another voice — the voice of the Lord. We can hear His words in that promise of

His, which shines like a bright light in the wilderness, as I mentioned earlier: "The Lord your God has led you in the wilderness that he might humble you and test you, to do you good in the end" (cf. Deuteronomy 8:2a,16b). And he spoke to me through a second verse, which I came to regard as being especially mine in this particular plight: "We call them happy because they endured. You have heard of Job's patience, and you know how the Lord provided for him in the end. For the Lord is full of mercy and compassion" (James 5:11 GNB). With these two verses God was saying to me that this desert-road experience of hitherto unanswered prayers was all part of His plan. The Father leads His children through the wilderness in order to test their trust. He wants to make them humble in the school of waiting. But the end He has prepared for them is good — the way will lead out of the wilderness into the wonderful land of Canaan.

When the voice of the Enemy tried to penetrate my heart during these troubles, as at other times of chastening, I opposed him with this Biblical truth: "God has prepared an outcome for these paths of chastening — a glorious one. He will do us good in the end." In prayer I reminded the Father of His promise again and again, taking my stand upon it, for His word is Yea and Amen. And, in fact, we experienced that God acts according to His word. Years later He provided a way out of our troubles in His love and mercy. His path of chastenings led out of the wilderness — just as He said it would — and into the land of promise, the prayed-for land, which we had already named Canaan.

God's grace shone upon us in a wonderful way

after the dark years of discipline. The building permit was unexpectedly granted. We could go ahead and purchase the neighbouring fields. God also helped us to pay each bill as it was due and then to develop and landscape the grounds. Now our little land of Canaan is a visible proof that paths of chastening end in joy and blessing, happiness and an abundance of good things from God's hand. If we heed His voice and what He says in His Word about chastening and suffering, we shall experience His overflowing goodness and see that all His promises are Yea and Amen. At that time my heart was filled with a deep longing in view of future paths of suffering: May we speak of discipline never as a punishment but as a grace. Then we shall see hardship unexpectedly transformed into something beneficial.

Today whenever we − and our fellow residents and visitors − walk across the little land of Canaan, we are filled with thanksgiving to see all the good and wonderful things the Lord has granted us. The houses, the grounds, a little Sea of Galilee (designed with the Holy Land in mind), the Garden of Jesus' Sufferings (a prayer garden depicting the Passion and Resurrection of Jesus with reliefs and inscriptions), but above all the Fountain of the Father's Goodness, declare that God is a Father of goodness and love, a Father of mercy. In a miraculous way He granted us an abundance of pure water, although the geological conditions could not have been less favourable for a boring.

Back then I discovered that our acceptance of divine chastenings or rebellion against them bears consequences not only for eternity, but for this life.

This I had learnt from the history of the people of Israel. All those among them who accepted the sufferings and chastenings in the wilderness entered the land of Canaan, a land flowing with milk and honey. God places the decision in our hands. The results of His discipline depend on us. Our attitude towards our cross has far-reaching effects, bringing us either misery and despair, or joy, blessing, and glory.

Yes, where do desert roads, paths of suffering and chastening lead to? Provided that we have the right attitude towards them, they will lead to an experience of God's goodness, often greater than before, to the bestowal of a very special gift that He has prepared for us in His love. This has nothing to do with pious talk or some petty consolation about suffering and chastening somehow having a bearable end. As sure as God is a loving Father, His fatherly heart cannot but bless us richly. For every path of chastening we have to follow He is constrained to grant us great joy and happiness — often in this life but even more so in heaven above, where we shall receive the fullness of joy and glory for all eternity.

Looking back, I can see what a wise and loving plan of God lay behind the many chastenings and sufferings in acquiring Canaan. In our Sisterhood we give thanks to Him ever anew for having led us through those years of discipline, which at the time seemed so long to us. Even while we were on this path, the Father let us experience His blessing — and not just later when He granted us Canaan, the wonderful outcome He had prepared for us. He enriched our lives spiritually. He taught and trained

13

us to humble ourselves beneath the divine blows and to submit to His will, immersing our will in His. And union with the will of God brings peace to the heart and joins us intimately to Him. This is the highest joy, and nothing can take it away from us.

How often we experienced on this path of discipline that our fervent prayers were not answered! — at least not at first. We had to struggle through in faith again and again. However, each new act of faith brings us closer to the heart of the Father; it leads us deeper into loving communion with the Father as a trusting child. And acts of faith forge us a crown.

On these paths of chastening God furthermore taught us to ask ourselves what the hindrances were that were keeping Him from answering our prayers. (Holy Scripture lists many examples of prayer hindrances.) He showed us that we ourselves were often at fault. By our attitude and conduct we were standing in the way of His goodness. When we repented and changed our ways and removed the hindrances — tensions and unlovingness, for instance — the way was free again and our prayers were answered. On these paths of discipline God granted us a deeper awareness of our sin and thus an ever-new repentance, which is the source of love for Jesus. Precious gifts lay in store for us on this path of discipline, which became a path of faith. What a wonderful and loving plan the Father had in leading us through these chastenings!

Before granting us the special gift of Canaan, the Father first wanted to remove the dross in us, since otherwise our uncleansed nature would have spoilt the good thing He had in store for us. Our land could never have become a true Canaan, a promised land of God, unless God had taken pains with us, the future residents, by disciplining us on this path and dealing with our unbelief, irreconciliation, self-will and everything else that opposes His will. Only if we underwent this cleansing process and were willing to be chastened — not just once but ever anew — could the Lord's joy, love and peace shine from this land through us.

And so we see that God in His love has our best interests at heart when He leads us into suffering and chastening. He wants us to become free and happy beings who, released from bondage to sin, can glorify Jesus with their lives. If we humble ourselves beneath the hand of God, we shall emerge from every chastening richly blessed and soon taste the fruit of suffering.

I was deeply struck by this fact for the first time when I began to write part of my life-story for my spiritual daughters in 1955. In retrospect, I could see, for instance, how the Lord had chastened me in my youth by letting me suffer great disappointments in someone. These disappointments made me very sad at the time; yes, I was almost inconsolable. This made me realize that this person, and not Jesus, was the centre of my life. I came to repentance and was kindled with the fervent plea that Jesus would be my first and foremost love. What was the outcome of this chastening? I came to know Jesus as the One who is worthy of our love as no one else is. Never before had I realized that it was possible to have such a personal relationship of love and dedication to Him. I became happier than before when my joy was centred on someone else.

15

This chastening brought me the greatest of all joys — Jesus became my first and foremost love.

A few years later I had a similar experience. During my college years when activities and popularity made me very much the centre of attention and I was in danger of letting this engross me, the Lord chastened me anew. He took me out of this happy circle and placed me in a group where as the youngest I had no say and where not much notice was taken of me. For quite a while He denied me the opportunity to get involved in satisfying activities. But again I experienced the truth of God's word, "to do you good in the end". The outcome He had prepared was a wonderful one. I experienced how He accepted my act of dedication and prayer to be released from the desire for rewarding activities and popularity. By means of these chastenings He made me independent of the praise and love of others. No longer did it matter to me whether I had a satisfying occupation or not. In Jesus I found complete satisfaction and He made me far happier than any satisfying activity could. To be loved by Him and to have His approval was now my heart's deep desire. I yearned to follow Him more closely, especially along the path of lowliness, and to be united with Him there. Thus once again the path of chastening brought me blessing upon blessing. In addition, God later led me into a field of activity that brought me much joy. How like our loving Father!

Yes, our paths of suffering and chastening are woven into a wonderful, eternal plan conceived in the loving heart of God the Father. He has carefully planned even the tiniest stretch along paths of chastening, bearing in mind the ultimate good of His child for both time and eternity. Our suffering will never weigh an ounce too much. He allows suffering to enter our lives, so that we might reap great joy, fruit and glory now and for all eternity — a blessed "afterwards".

God will be honoured and His name as Father will be glorified when we consider how He has chastened us and think of the fruit, joy and blessing His chastenings have brought us. In a time of quiet we may find it a help to write down the paths of chastening in one column and the outcome in an adjacent column. Our eyes will be opened to see God as the all-powerful Father, who has only good things in store for us on paths of discipline and who loves us immeasurably. This recollection will also strengthen us for the coming hardships that we shall no doubt have to endure in the end times.

A Chance to Become a New Person

A good father loves his child and cares about its well-being and happiness, always thinking of ways to bring it joy. If this is true of an earthly father, how much more so of our heavenly Father, "from whom all fatherhood in heaven and on earth derives its name" (Ephesians 3:15 NIV). But if He demonstrates this goodness mostly in times of chastening, this must probably be the only way in which we can receive it. Otherwise God, who loves us dearly, would find another way of showing us His goodness. God knows that the real source of our unhappiness is our sinful nature, our sinning — a fact we so often forget. If the Father wishes to make us happy here on earth and later for all eternity, He has to deal with our sins.

Sin in itself is an affliction and a punishment. As Scripture says, sin is a people's ruin (cf. Proverbs 14:34). This has become terrifyingly evident with the upsurge of sin ever since the commandments of God were disregarded and lawlessness became widespread. Sexual perversion, alcoholism and drug addiction with their terrible side-effects are on the advance, leaving many damaged lives in their wake. At a medical conference as early as 1972 it was stated that eleven million persons were currently suffering from venereal disease as a result of sexual permissiveness. If a sinful life can destroy a person's body in this world, what horrors must he endure in the world to come! So, ultimately, it is a mark of God's love when He judges and chastens those who commit such sins. For instance, He may let them fall ill or be committed to a mental institution. Hard leadings like these have jolted people out of their sinful way of life before it was too late. In their great distress they have learnt to call upon Jesus and found Him as their Redeemer. They were saved and healed and became truly happy.

May it go deep into our hearts that when God chastens us He is showing us the greatest love: He wishes to rouse us from our indifference and laxity towards sin. Sometimes we tolerate sin in our lives without even realizing it, because we have grown accustomed to our sin and do not reckon with the fact that it always leads to misery. A real problem among us believers is that we often fail to take sin seriously. We argue that we are redeemed by the blood of Jesus. But he who truly believes in Jesus as his Saviour will take sin seriously because of the high price Jesus paid for its expiation.

It is a dangerous thing to think we can sit back and rest as far as our sins are concerned just because we have undergone infant baptism, conversion, baptism by immersion or baptism in the Spirit. Whoever thinks that he can enter God's kingdom of glory without fighting against his sins or without the readiness to undergo chastening, has unwittingly fallen into the Enemy's clutches. Yes, he has fallen prey to a dangerous delusion. Holy Scripture teaches believers differently – namely, through chastening we shall partake of God's holiness (cf. Hebrews 12:10).

Satan, however, does everything he can to make us treat sin lightly. Then we do not resist it with all our might; we are unwilling to be chastened and purified. And the outcome? By remaining in our sins, we become unhappy; Satan gains power over us, and we are barred from entering the kingdom of God. Knowing all this, Satan tries to blind us to our sins and to make us excuse them, so that we no longer think it wrong if we, as believers, continue in so-called little sins. Perhaps we argue in our blindness, "It's my strained nerves that make me get so upset." – or: "Sometimes you just have to speak your mind. You can't take everything lying down." But the truth is that we are angry, fault-finding, bitter, rebellious in our words and actions, quarrelsome and unforgiving, forgetting that those who do

19

such things "shall not inherit the kingdom of God", as Scripture says (Galatians 5:20f.).

Yet even if we are blind to our sins, God is not. And in His love He does not want us to die in our sins, that is, reap misery in this life and eternal condemnation later because of our sins, which give the Enemy a claim to us. Desiring to protect us from this, God begins to chasten us, so that sin cannot continue to flourish in us and make us unhappy as we suffer its effects.

No doubt, we have all tasted the consequences of sin. For example, we are filled with bitterness, unable to forgive another person — and what happens? We are dejected, inwardly torn and perhaps unable to sleep at night. Or envy and selfish ambition gnaw at our hearts. We forget how fortunate we are and, instead of feeling grateful for all that we have been given, we look at others enviously, thinking that they are somehow more favoured than we. As a result our joy disappears. Sin is always our ruin, whether it be jealousy, lying, pride or impurity or some other sin that we harbour. Sin binds us to Satan, the foe of human happiness. He incites us to sin, in order to rob us of our joy.

Could there be a greater love than that of our heavenly Father? Our happiness means so much to Him that He chastens us in order to free us from these sins. God the Father wants to see His children happy. Indeed, Jesus saved us so that joy would be ours. This is why He says, "No one will take your joy from you" (John 16:22). He wants to give us this joy — especially on paths of cross-bearing, on paths of chastening, where His saving power is to be worked out in our lives, bringing us release from our sins and letting us share His holiness. With deep gratitude the Apostle Paul testifies to the saving grace of God, for "by it we are disciplined to renounce godless ways and worldly desires, and to live a life of temperance, honesty, and godliness" (Titus 2:12 NEB).

Of the many chastenings that I have experienced in my life, I can only say that God has sent them to me in His fatherly love in order to release me from my sinful traits and make me a happy person. And so it is for chastenings that I have to thank Him the most in my life. Yes, I must confess that the reason why I have become so happy is that on paths of chastening the Lord has dealt with the various sinful areas in my life.

I recall that many years ago there were times when I became dejected and unhappy because I was either jealous, over-sensitive and irritable or because I felt hurt and resentful when wronged. Then the Lord began to chasten me. He let me experience disappointments in others. He brought me together with a difficult person, whom He repeatedly used to deal blows to the hard and sinful part in me in order to extract love from my heart. As I became painfully aware of my sinful bondage to bitterness, I learnt to cry to Jesus, my Redeemer, that He might release me from this — and He did so. It was His chastening that evoked in me this fervent plea, which the Lord then answered. He granted me the grace to forgive and to be merciful and I was released from my unhappy state.

Another sin lay hidden in my heart at the time — and that was pride. I found it hard to bear when I was unfairly treated and slandered, my reputation ruined. Whenever this happened, my heart swelled with indignation at such lies and injustices. The Lord saw this proud and hard area in my heart and knew that it was preventing me from being happy. As the loving Father that He is, He began to discipline and chasten me. After the founding of our Sisterhood, a real slander campaign was launched, bringing with it many injustices and humiliations for the Sisterhood and, in particular, for myself.

This was how the heavenly Father disciplined me. It was He who raised up the adversaries whose arrows, figuratively speaking, pierced the hard and proud part of my heart. Since there were very many arrows over the years, the hard part in my heart was increasingly punctured and Jesus poured in more and more of His love until I had really learnt to love my adversaries.

Scarcely a day goes by without my giving thanks to the Father for this painful path of chastening. Why? Because happy is he who can love and remain at peace instead of getting worked up when he is hurt, spitefully treated or wronged. I cannot say what deep joy pathways of chastening have brought me. Yet this is inevitable, seeing that chastenings come from our loving Father in heaven, who gives us only good things.

I am reminded of one of our Sisters who some time ago came to me, radiant with happiness. She had been due to receive her final consecration at a special service, but then it was cancelled for her. This was a deep humiliation and a very painful experience for her − a chastening from God. However, she accepted God's chastening wholeheartedly. And as she then shared with me, "I am so happy. On this path of chastening I have experienced a deep renewal in my heart." This joy would not have entered her life if God had not chastened and disciplined her but left her as she was. She experienced a blessed "afterwards". Chastenings bring forth abundant joy — a fruit of righteousness. As the Psalmist sings: "Blessed is the man whom thou dost chasten, O Lord!" (Psalm 94:12).

In the Face of Eternity

Perhaps some will be familiar with the legend of a man who, after working in the Lord's service, arrived at the gates of heaven when his life was over. An angel presented him with a big, shining, golden nugget as the fruit of his labours on earth. Overjoyed, the man exclaimed, "Thanks be to God! What glorious fruit for eternity!" Then the angel took away the nugget in order to have its components examined. When he returned, all that was left was a tiny grain. The man was indignant. "That can't be true! How can such a tiny grain be the fruit of my entire life? I have served the Lord untiringly!" he protested. "Only that which is done and sacrificed out of pure love for Jesus counts as fruit in eternity," came the angel's reply.

The Lord, wishing to spare us such disappointments in eternity, chastens us in this life, so that our love for Jesus will become pure and sincere. For instance, He may let us experience no success in our work, only disappointments, if much of what we have done was out of selfish ambition or for our personal satisfaction. He wants to teach us to do our service out of love for Him with no ulterior motive.

With our eternal destiny at heart, God in His fatherly love for us is concerned that we learn all this here on earth. And so He applies the pruning knife without sparing us and often leads us along difficult paths of chastening. He has something in mind that we usually fail to consider. Our life on earth will soon come to an end, to be followed by our real life in the next world, where we shall live and abide for ever. During these brief years on earth the die is cast as to whether we shall then be taken to a place of everlasting joy and happiness or to a place of misery and torment. Our eternal destiny is determined now. Do we believe in Jesus as our Redeemer and do we prove the genuineness of our faith and dedication by letting the Father train, chasten and judge us? Or do we evade His hand? Again, the die is cast in this life. Either we are willing to be made fit for His heavenly kingdom or else we inwardly resist chastenings and paths of suffering by grumbling, complaining and rebelling, and as a result find ourselves standing outside His kingdom one day.

By inward resistance towards sufferings and chastenings, we hinder God's work, preventing Him from purifying and transforming our nature. Our specific sins continue to have a hold on us and so does the Enemy. At the end of our life Satan can assert his right to us if as believers we have persisted in bitterness, strife, irreconciliation, carnal desires, lying, slander, and other sins. (Galatians

5:19-21; Ephesians 5:3-5). As the Accuser he will refuse us entrance into the kingdom of God.

Each one of us who has not humbled himself beneath the chastening of God will personally come under judgment — and we shall be judged by Him in the same measure that we evaded His chastening hand in this life.

According to Holy Scripture, this judgment and condemnation of God can also include punishment in hell, as for example in the cases of the unmerciful servant (Matthew 18:34) and the wicked servant who complained that his master was a hard man (Matthew 25:30). Yes, Jesus warns even His followers of incurring the punishment of hell. Can we imagine what hell must be like? When thinking about the terrible things that happen in our world, how often we say, "It's a hell!" But nothing on earth can compare with the real hell. Jesus repeatedly reminds us that the conditions in hell will be more horrible than words can express. There people will suffer the most agonizing torments. The cries of horror, the wailing and weeping will have no end. This is a kingdom ruled by Satan, who as the personification of malice and sadism takes delight in tormenting those who enter his kingdom. If not there, then in the realm of the dead, a person will have to suffer punishment for his particular sins if he did not repent of them, confess them, and bring them to Jesus to be washed away in His blood, and if he did not break with his sinful ways.

What grace that there is a redemption from sin, a cleansing of sin through the blood of Jesus! What grace that the Lord continues His work of transformation in us by leading us along paths of chastening so as to prune away our sins and make us fit to share His holiness! Jesus regards the horrors of hell and the immeasurable sufferings that await people there as being so agonizing that He warns His disciples, "Do not fear those who kill the body but cannot kill the soul; rather fear him who can destroy both soul and body in hell" (Matthew 10:28). By this He declares that all chastenings, all sufferings, yes, even death by torture, are nothing in comparison to the agonies that one must endure in hell. And so we should judge everything by the right standards. All earthly sufferings and chastenings are to be considered as trivial. Only that which awaits us in eternity should be important to us. For eternity is never-ending. It cannot be measured in terms of time. All our sufferings and chastenings on earth will soon be over and therefore they cannot compare with the sufferings of the realm of the dead, let alone hell.

From this viewpoint we can understand why God sends us chastenings in this short lifetime and why He makes every effort to prepare us by means of chastenings for the heavenly glory, His kingdom of joy. God in His love does not want us to stand condemned one day and be banished to the kingdom of death or hell.

In the next world we would, humanly speaking, bitterly reproach God if we were shut out from His kingdom for ever and confined to some region in the realm of the dead or even hell itself just because He had not led us along paths of chastening. How dreadful it would be if at the end of our lives we had to hear from Jesus' lips the terrible words, "Depart from Me!" because we persisted in an unforgiving attitude, bitterness, envy and other sins! Yes, we would blame God for not loving us, since otherwise He would have sent us chastenings to spare us such pain in eternity. Thus we can see that chastenings are actually tokens of God's love, since they are meant to keep us from eternal sufferings and prepare us for eternal joys — joys without end.

Indeed, our heavenly Father in His love wants at all costs to spare His own the same fate as the unbelieving world — judgment and condemnation in eternity. And so we read in Holy Scripture, "When we are judged by the Lord, we are chastened so that we may not be condemned along with the world" (1 Corinthians 11:32). For all eternity we shall thank the Father for His paths of chastening, since they are "blows of love" intended to prepare us. They help to transform us into His image, making us all light, so that we might dwell with Him for ever in His kingdom of light, peace and joy.

Yet how great our anguish would be after death if the Father had to show us in the next world how He sought to bring about something very wonderful in us through one chastening or the other but in vain, since we resisted His discipline with complaints and grumbling! In the next world it will be too late — too late to make up for lost opportunities. We shall stand there, sad and pathetic, unable to enter the heavenly glory, since the transformation that was to be wrought in us through chastenings had not been effected.

How much depends on our saying "Yes, Father" to paths of suffering and chastening — and not just once but ever anew. For if the chastening is especially hard, a single act of dedication to the Father will not suffice. This act needs to be renewed again and again so that the chastening will bring us the fruit of glory in the next world. However, we shall attain the goal of heavenly glory if we continue to trust in the redemptive power of Jesus' blood and at the same time willingly submit to His chastening. These two, faith and acceptance of chastenings, are inseparably bound up with each other if we wish to partake of His holiness and inherit the kingdom of glory prepared for us.

Whoever bears eternity in mind can endure chastenings in the right spirit and will emerge victorious. The sufferings and chastenings of this present time seem small to him. They are not permanent. Only that which lasts for ever is of importance to him — eternity with its boundless joy or immeasurable torment.

In a hymn Gerhard Tersteegen once described our life on earth as being "only a pathway". A pathway leads somewhere. It brings us to our destination. And in this case our final destination is eternity. Would we follow a smooth path if we knew that it leads us to a gruesome place of suffering instead of a wonderful place of joy and happiness? No, we would prefer the rough and stony path, in spite of its many obstacles and the sweat it costs us, for it brings us to the goal of everlasting happiness. It is written of Jesus that in the midst of disgrace He looked to "the joy that was set before him" (Hebrews 12:2), and that gave Him the strength to endure.

What gives us the strength to bear chastenings in the right spirit? What helps us to say Yes to them in this short life on earth? The prospect of eternity.

Heaven is a reality, and so too the kingdom of death and hell. Depending on the life we have lived here, we shall be received into the kingdom of death and darkness or into the kingdom of light and glory for all eternity. The choice is ours.

Eternity is the only thing that matters. There we shall see that it was chastenings that brought us joy and happiness for ever more — provided we accepted them from God's hand. Yes, he who yearns for joy and happiness will want to ensure his joy for all eternity. As a prudent man, as a realist, he will want to make his eternal home in the place where this joy will be his. And so in his short time on earth he will have a wholehearted Yes to paths of chastening and suffering. Did we always have a Yes? In times of quiet when we come before the Lord, let us search our hearts. How did we react to divine chastenings? What was our attitude towards them? Did we give God our Yes?

It is indescribable how much we gain from chastenings, how much fruit and joy we reap from them, if we give God our Yes. This begins even in the present life when the promises of Holy Scripture come true: "Afterwards it yields the peaceable fruit of righteousness" (Hebrews 12:11 RAV) and He will "do you good in the end" (Deuteronomy 8:16b). And in the next world happiness will cling to the soles of our feet and everlasting joy will be upon our heads (cf. Isaiah 35:10). Yes, in the heavenly glory we shall be satisfied with joy for ever. And so the sufferings in this life, including all chastenings, "are not worth comparing with the glory that is to be revealed to us" (Romans 8:18).

In the heart of God our Father every stretch of our pathway has been lovingly conceived. And so when God takes such pains with us and disciplines us by leading us along difficult paths, it is a mark of His great goodness. Whoever is a father or mother knows how difficult it is to deal with the same fault over and over again when bringing up a child. How painfully frustrating it is when the child is unruly and defiant, constantly misbehaving! Time and again the parents are forced to discipline it. But their hearts ache. They can hardly bring themselves to continue such measures. It is an effort for them to go on believing that a change will still come over their child. And so they often have to struggle with themselves before they can go on disciplining their child, trying first this method, then that. But they do so in the hope that their child will benefit from the chastening. The love of true parents never tires of bringing up their child. The heavenly Father, from whom all fatherhood derives its name, imparts this untiring love to earthly, human fathers as a trait of His fatherly nature. But how great this untiring love must be in our heavenly Father Himself, who has the difficult task of bringing us up as His children!

Usually, we see only what the paths of chastening cost us. This is why Holy Scripture exhorts us, "Remember that the Lord your God corrects and punishes you just as a father disciplines his children" (Deuteronomy 8:5 GNB). And disciplining means hard work. At times everyone rearing a child feels like dropping everything and letting the child go its own way, since the task brings too many struggles, disappointments and wounds, too much suffering. Our heavenly Father takes all this upon Himself when He raises us. So often when He tries to bring us up and chastens us, we wound Him with our resistance, making Him lament, "You burdened me with your sins; you wore me out with the wrongs you committed!" (Isaiah 43:24 GNB). In the New Testament we read how Jesus lamented over His disciples, "How long am I to bear with you?" (Mark 9:19). Nonetheless, the Lord does not give us up or leave us to our fate. Tireless in His love, He continues to chasten us, ever willing to take upon Himself the suffering involved.

That true parents are ever anew prepared to discipline their unruly children is understandable. That no amount of pain and trouble is too much for them is also understandable. For as they themselves have to conclude, "The children have inherited many of our negative qualities. They are sinful just as we are. They are our own flesh and blood." But God in His holiness knows no sin. He hates it. It is an abomination to Him. How much it must therefore cost Him to deal with our sins the whole time! Could anything be more distressing? Long ago God lamented over His impenitent people, who did not want to turn from their sins, "They are a burden that I am tired of bearing" (Isaiah 1:14 GNB). How very deep the Father's love for us must be if in spite of all the suffering our sin causes Him, He does not grow weary of disciplining and chastening us! He endures all this so that we might partake of the divine nature and become truly happy, free from the power of sin.

Even more amazing is the fact that the Father delivered up His dearly beloved Son into the hands of sinners to be crucified for our redemption. This is the proof that His discipline and chastening are motivated by love alone. Otherwise He would not have allowed His Son to undergo this immeasurable suffering. So when chastened by God, we can only reply, even though it may be with tears, "Father, I thank You for Your chastenings, which are an expression of Your great love for me! You do not wish to give me up to my sinning or abandon me to misery. You want to cleanse and purify me and transform me into Your image, so that for time and eternity I shall be a happy person, showing forth the victory of Jesus."

Yes, praise and thanksgiving to the Father! Though He created the entire universe and guides it according to His eternal plan, He takes a very personal interest in each one of us. For each one of us He has planned the right help with a path of chastening just suited to us. He wants to make happy people of us, free from the power of sin. And even though at first we often resist and rebel against God's love and His wise upbringing, God the Father does not stop bringing us up. He knows the sinful areas of our nature better than we do. Some may be touchy, hot-tempered, self-indulgent, domineering, self-willed; whereas others are untruthful, servile, vain, always finding fault with others, apathetic or self-centred.

Our heavenly Father now wants to help us to become free from these sins, which not only make us unhappy in this life but bring us great anguish for eternity. He begins to chasten us and apply the pruning knife to these sinful parts in our natures. At the same time He lovingly bears in mind that one child will reach the goal only through a particular chastening, whereas another child needs a completely different path of chastening. And so I would gain nothing from enduring someone else's hardships. With my particular sinful disposition I would never reach the goal God has set me, for these blows would not strike at my specific faults. Since God alone knows what the sinful areas in my life are, the blows and chastenings He allows to befall me are the sole and proper means of help for me.

To this end He may use a difficult person whom He brings into our lives. A man of God once said, "It's worth paying a fortune for a difficult person to come from the ends of the earth, for he does us an invaluable service." Such a person is an instrument of God and renders us the greatest service of all: he teaches us to love. When brought together with such a person, we realize that we are incapable of loving or even forgiving him. In this way God confronts us with our sin, so that we battle against it in faith. He uses this difficult person like a whetstone to purge us of our sin, because He wants to see us happy. And happy is he who can love others, including those who make life difficult for him. The kingdom of heaven belongs to those who love God and who can therefore love their neighbour and bear with him, that is forgive him, not holding a grudge against him or growing embittered. Such people are happy already in this life, and above, in

Jesus' kingdom, they will know joy beyond compare, having overcome all touchiness, resentment, anger, bitterness, etc. For as it is written, "he who overcomes shall inherit all things" (Revelation 21:7 RAV).

Who can say how much benefit and blessing come from difficult paths of chastening! We can never thank our heavenly Father enough for taking such pains with our upbringing. The ways He leads us are many and varied, but they all pertain to our highest good. Such love is beyond understanding.

I am reminded of how God led a schoolfriend of mine. In earlier years when I spoke to her about the Lord Jesus, she showed no interest. But the Father in heaven saw that she was in danger of forfeiting her eternal salvation for the sake of her earthly happiness, which she clung to. Later she said to me, "Whenever you spoke to me about Jesus and said that I should give my life to Him, I was always afraid that Jesus might take my husband away from me." Her husband meant everything to her, and for this reason she did not want to surrender her life to Jesus.

What did the heavenly Father do so that she would find true happiness? In His love He chastened her. One day her husband was suddenly taken from her by a fatal car accident. This tragedy plunged her into deep anguish, and at first the future seemed like one great aching void. Meaninglessness stared her in the face. But then she found Jesus and committed her whole life to Him. Now she says, "I am so happy, much happier than before when I still had my husband!" Incomprehensible though it may seem, this painful chastening brought her overwhelming joy – not only for this lifetime but for all eternity. After pain and grief she experienced a blessed "afterwards", according to His promise "to do you good in the end".

Can we sense how much the Father's thoughts are taken up with us? He plans the right pathway for each one of us, deciding which events, people, sufferings and illnesses are to come into our lives, all with the aim of training us, so that we shall be prepared for happiness in this life and in eternity. Yet where does He find children who thank Him for this difficult task? As we shall see one day in eternity, we can never thank our Father enough for chastening and disciplining us in spite of our ingratitude, and for not growing weary of His task or giving us up although we cause Him so much trouble and effort with our sins. Do we not have every reason to pray when humbled: "I thank You for humbling me, for then You exalt me. I thank You for taking away what I wanted to keep, for You will give me something far greater in return. I thank You for bringing that difficult person into my life, for this is a sign that You want to free me from my sin of unlovingness. I thank You for doing Your utmost to lead me on to the goal of glory."

A Hard Love, the Greatest Love

Paths of suffering, paths of chastening – what great transformation, grace and blessing they can bring to a person's life! But they can also have the opposite effect. They can lead us into misery, make us bitter and dejected, and drive us to despair. Chastenings are not in themselves sufficient to do us good. What counts is a person's reaction and attitude towards them. Whether we become happy people in this world and the next, and whether we partake of His holiness, depends on us.

Our attitude towards chastening and suffering corresponds to our heart-attitude towards God. Is our relationship with God that of a child or of a servant? Our reaction to chastenings will accordingly be positive or negative. A child brought up by loving parents expects good things from its father. Yes, even if it is too small to understand its father's actions, it still trusts in his love when, for instance, the father removes the child from the security of home and takes it to a hospital where, far away from its family, it undergoes painful treatment. But how different is the attitude of a servant! When a servant cannot understand his master's actions, which to him seem hard and painful, he attributes the master's dealings to harshness. He is likely to be bitter and rebellious, saying, "I'll just have to put up with it." As far as a servant is concerned, his master is just that and nothing more. He does not think of him as a father.

God is our Father — that is, He becomes our Father when we believe in Jesus Christ. But the question is: Are we true children of His; do we have the attitude of a child towards Him? A small child does not need to understand its father, for it knows that it is loved. This knowledge gives the child a feeling of security and deep comfort even when the father punishes it. Because a child trusts its father's love, it can submit to the will and dealings of the father. But in our hearts the servant strives with the child. We must first become like children again, as Jesus says, for just as we have been redeemed by Jesus that we might show forth His redemption in our lives, so have we become God's children by faith in Jesus' atoning death in order that we would become children in the truest sense of the word and act like children towards Him. And this we have to learn again.

Yes, our firm goal of faith should be, "I shall not let You go until You have made me a child again, small and trusting!" Then we shall experience what the Bible says, "To such belongs the kingdom of God" (Mark 10:14) – that is, they are happy. True children of the heavenly Father have no contrary opinions or questions. They do not know how to do everything better. They do not make a problem of everything. No, as trusting children, they are fully surrendered to all that the Father might do with them, having the assurance deep down in their hearts, "My Father knows everything. He can do everything and is always right. My Father is good. My Father loves me!" Accordingly, they accept chastenings from their Father's hand as a matter of course. They are conscious of their smallness, and so they say, "We know nothing. We don't really understand anything. We are not able to judge matters. But the Father can. He alone understands everything." And they humbly leave everything to Him.

If this is how a good-natured little child behaves towards its earthly father, how can our relationship to our heavenly Father be any different? Let us consider who our Father in heaven is. The eternal, immortal, almighty God, with whom none can compare, Maker of heaven and earth. And who are we? We sing in a hymn, "Our knowledge and understanding are shrouded in darkness…" How can we pitiful, sinful creatures with our so limited perception fathom the purposes and plans of God, which are as deep and as wide as eternity? How can a sinful mortal being understand the great and holy, eternal God? God would not be God if we could understand Him. But God saved us through Jesus so that we might be sons of God, and as such we can nevertheless understand Him — with a loving, child-like trust.

So be a child and say, "My Father, I trust You and know that however hard Your chastening may be, it is only for my good. On this path You have blessings in store for me." Say again and again, "My Father, my Father, I'm Your child! A father won't let his child perish when the going is rough. Nor will You let me perish in my hardships, but bring me through this time of chastening. You have prepared a way out of my distress!" And when His pathway almost seems to lead you into an abyss and you are in danger of rebelling against His will because it seems too hard and incomprehensible to you, then say: "My Father, I do not understand You, but I trust You. My Father, even though my heart is almost breaking on this difficult pathway, I'm filled with trust, for I know that You have a wonderful purpose behind it all. This purpose, which was conceived in Your loving heart, cannot be anything but wonderful, and You will accomplish it gloriously. Yes, I believe that in Your fatherly love You are leading me on to a wonderful goal. I know You cannot do otherwise. And I believe what You say to me in Your Word: 'My thoughts are not your thoughts, neither are your ways my ways…For as the heavens are higher than the earth, so are my ways higher than your ways and my thoughts than your thoughts' (Isaiah 55:8f.). Knowing this, I want to humble myself as befits a little child and lovingly submit to Your mighty hand when You discipline me."

Whoever responds like this allows the Spirit of God to make him more and more like a child. And the servant within him is driven out — that part of his nature which rebels against hard leadings of God and divine chastenings. Paths of chastening, as he will discover, will not lead him into a state of despair and embitterment but bring him to the very heart of God. Moreover, he will experience that trust and dedication to the Father's will not only deprive suffering of its power; they fill the heart with peace and great comfort, yes, divine joy. He will actually taste the kingdom of heaven, joy, peace, and the Father's love, just as Jesus promised us if we become children. But if we have a servant's attitude, if we chafe at God's will in defiance, we shall experience great unhappiness along paths of suffering and chastening. When we set our will against God's will, we forfeit all the good things God wanted to grant us on paths of chastening. Our defiance is a barrier impeding the flow.

It is up to us whether we have a foretaste of heaven in this life — particularly during and following times of chastening — or whether we grow frustrated because we think we have too much to bear.

God, for His part, has resolved to give us good things through these chastenings. But whether we receive them or not depends on our decision.

In God we have a loving Father, who brings us up as His children, for by virtue of Jesus' redemption we sinful and wicked beings are permitted to be sons of God. What a wonderful gift that is! When I consider that in all our leadings, including the painful ones, we are guided by the Father's will, I can only stand in awe and wonder. How privileged we are! We are not at the mercy of some tyrant. Rather we have the very best and wisest father there is! To Him we can say, "How wonderful that I may know You, my Father! Your will is goodness and Your heart is nothing but loving-kindness. And I know that all Your leadings are good for me."

Chastenings reveal whether our relationship to God is that of a child or of a servant. Holy Scripture explicitly says that only those who are led by the Spirit of God are sons of God. The Spirit of God, however, is a spirit of affirmation, prompting us to say Yes to God and His will. If we cannot bear chastenings, but are rebellious, embittered, dejected or fall into despair, we are saying No to the will of God and demonstrating that we are a servant and not a child. Such an attitude calls for repentance. Dark times of affliction and disaster lie ahead of us, and so everything depends on our now becoming children in our relationship to God. Otherwise we shall not be able to endure the future and shall fall into despair. But then we shall have only ourselves to blame, because in former times of chastening we acted like a mere servant towards Him, as if He were a stranger. We were meant to know Him as our Father, who has proved His love for us by sacrificing His only begotten Son. If only we would believe that this same love is behind every chastening in our lives! Then we would be strong in the coming times of hardship.

Too Late

From the history of Israel, which has been set as an example of God's ways and dealings with His own, we can see that there can also be a "too late" on paths of chastening. The Lord waited 23 years before letting His judgment descend upon Israel with the destruction of Jerusalem and the Babylonian captivity. For 23 years God warned His people through the Prophet Jeremiah and led them along various paths of chastening and discipline (Jeremiah 25:3). But then came the hour when His loving admonishments and chastenings, having been rejected, turned into anguished wrath; and a terrible judgment descended upon Israel. The fact that God waited 23 years before carrying out His judgment shows how great His love and patience are as He wrestles for our souls on paths of chastening.

This is why the Lord entreated His people, "If you will return, O Israel, return to me...Circumcise yourselves to the Lord, circumcise your hearts...or my wrath will break out and burn like fire because of the evil you have done" (Jeremiah 4:1,4 NIV). In this summons of the Lord lies His appeal to us that we mend our ways in response to chastening, so that He will not have to express His wrath and send judgment upon us. But when we refuse to heed His admonishments and chastenings, when we do not mend our ways, He is forced to be wrathful. How immeasurably hard this must be for Him! In the Book of Jeremiah God expresses, as it were, one last hope of reaching His people: "It may be they will listen, and every one turn from his evil way" (Jeremiah 26:3).

In His love God does not tire of warning us and bringing us up, for He does not want us to reach the too-late point in our lives. This He wants to avoid at all costs, for then there will be no more opportunity for us to be set right on paths of chastening and to turn over a new leaf. And then the hour of judgment will strike. Time and again this has been demonstrated in people's personal lives and in the history of mankind.

It is shattering to think that with the dawn of the end times, the era of God's wrath is being ushered in and the time of His patience is drawing to an end. His countenance and that of the Lamb will change. The countenance of grace will turn into the countenance of wrath, and people will cry out to the mountains and rocks, "Fall on us and hide us from the face of him who is seated on the throne, and from the wrath of the Lamb" (Revelation 6:16). On that day, the day of God's wrath, mankind — godless, enslaved to sin and Satan, defiant towards God — will experience even here on earth that "God is a consuming fire" (Hebrews 12:29). They will discover that "it is a fearful thing to fall into the hands of the living God" (Hebrews 10:31). The waves of God's wrath will roll over the earth as Revelation tells us. When a world-wide disaster triggered off by a nuclear war hits the earth, one wave of death and devastation will follow the other.

We are standing on the threshold of this era. Because of the extent of its sin mankind is ripe for judgment — that is, mankind will incur God's wrath, and terrible judgments will descend, causing millions to cry out in despair. But then their clamouring will be too late, since all God's warnings and disciplinary measures were lost upon them.

Even as believers we can incur God's judgment if we have rebelled against His chastenings and warnings and they have failed to have an effect on us. As Christians we know Jesus as our personal Saviour and Helper. We have experienced the love of God and know that His discipline is inspired by His fatherly goodness and that when He leads us on paths of chastening it is an act of grace. But if in spite of this we have grumbled in our hearts against chastenings and have not accepted them, one day it will be too late for us. This means that the Lord will encounter us no longer as our loving Father, who admonishes His child and seeks to bring it up by means of this chastening or that. No, He will come to us as Judge in His holy wrath. Then we shall no longer be under His grace and love as before when God chastened and disciplined us as His child.

In the life of His people Israel we see the shattering reality of the two countenances of God, to which the prophets refer time and again. We see the countenance of grace when God in His fatherly love protected His people, let them experience His miracles and loving guidance on paths of chastening — as during the years of wandering through the wilderness. And we see the countenance of wrath when God turned from His people and let terrible judgments take their course. They were delivered into the hands of their enemies and sent into captivity. Terror, destruction and death struck. Woe betide us if we, like many of His people in the wilderness long ago, rebel against God as He lovingly chastens us and brings us up. Then the hour will come when God has to turn His countenance against us in wrath. Woe betide us if we are judged and condemned along with the world in the age of God's wrath. What does this entail? Untold misery, which begins already here on earth. The holy God is not to be mocked. He hates sin and punishes it.

And what is the most deeply rooted sin? Rebellion against God. This is the sin of Lucifer and it is satanic. Expulsion from the presence of God and severe judgment will follow if we do not repent and bring our sins to Jesus, who will cleanse us with His blood. Whoever keeps on resisting God's disciplinary measures and rebelling against Him is like the wicked servant who said to his master, "You are a hard man." And he will have to share the same fate: "Cast the worthless servant into the outer darkness" (Matthew 25:30).

Do we realize to what extent we are affected by our attitude towards chastenings? This will become evident not only in eternity but in this life, as we shall discover in the end-time era, the age of God's wrath. The Lord has told us what to expect in the end times so that we would be aware of the reality of His judgments of wrath, their implication for us and the world, and prepare ourselves accordingly.

Just as long ago Jesus forewarned His people about the judgments that would befall the city of Jerusalem, so He has clearly told us about the judgments that will mark the close of the age. He has accurately described the end-time characteristics, which are now becoming a reality before our eyes. He has admonished and entreated us, saying, "Watch at all times, praying that you may have strength to escape all these things that will take place, and to stand before the Son of man" (Luke 21:36). We are reminded of the rapture, which will take place before the terrible sufferings of the antichristian era reach their peak. Those who belong to Jesus and who have been transformed into His image along paths of chastening will be caught up to Him. Holy Scripture says, "Strive for…holiness without which no one will see the Lord" (Hebrews 12:14). And so we shall be taken up to meet Jesus and behold Him face to face only if we have become partakers of God's holiness by allowing Him to do His refining work in us along paths of divine discipline.

Even in the present time, which is not the antichristian era proper, but only preliminary to it, everything depends on whether we allow ourselves to be refined through chastenings. We are living in a time when fears and perils abound, even though a nuclear war has not yet broken out. We are threatened by crime and violence, threatened by revolutionary movements, threatened by pollution and the contamination of the earth, threatened by persecutions — yes, threatened on every side!

But those who humbled themselves beneath the mighty hand of God and submitted to His chastening are, as it were, lifted out of the fears and hardships. Though weeping, they said Yes to the will of God, and this united them with His heart. They learnt to immerse their will completely in His. And so they are one with God. In the midst of fears and dangers they rest in His heart, where they find comfort and security. What grace God's paths of chastening and purification have brought them for these hard times, which we have to go through now, and later for the far greater trials and hardships that the end-time judgments will bring mankind! "The Lord knows how to rescue the godly from trial" (2 Peter 2:9). Time and again we read words like these in the Bible. The godly, according to the messages to the seven churches, are the overcomers, whom the Lord will deliver out of the hour of trial that will come upon the whole world (cf. Revelation 3:10).

In other words, it is possible to be delivered out of the hour of great judgment when the anguished wrath of God is poured out upon the earth. For God delights in grace, not judgment. He who submits to chastening and judgment now has already been judged for his sins and does not need to be judged by God along with the world when the divine judgment of wrath descends upon a godless humanity.

How important, therefore, are the paths of chastening by which the Lord leads His own! In His love God the Father makes every effort to prepare them by means of chastenings, so that they will not have to taste the full measure of the coming horrors. He wants to spare and protect them in the actual age of wrath. In Revelation 9:4, for instance, it says that those who have the seal of God on their foreheads could not be harmed by the terrible plague of locusts. Accordingly, the Lord chastens us now, so that He need not judge us along with the world. Since God does not wish to pour out His wrath upon us, mankind, He does everything to bring us to repentance. He takes great pains with us, warning us ever anew and sending various chastenings. In view of future events He calls us to repent and walk in holiness – an appeal conveyed, for instance, by the Apostle Peter, who in his letter also refers to the divine judgments of wrath that will descend at the close of the age. Paths of chastening, as Holy Scripture says, make us partakers of God's holiness and cause His image to be formed in us, so that by our lives we can show that we belong to Him.

There are times of grace and times of wrath. Over and over again the Lord speaks of this. We are under the grace of God and experiencing a time of grace when He chastens and disciplines us. But if we have not accepted chastenings, we are headed for a time of wrath. For then we too shall come under the divine judgment of wrath, which will soon descend upon the world. Or we shall be faced with the consuming fire of God's wrath when we enter the next world.

Israel was under divine grace when God said, "I solemnly warned your fathers when I brought them up out of the land of Egypt, warning them persistently, even to this day, saying, Obey my voice" (Jeremiah 11:7). Yet they caused God to lament, "I punished you, but it did no good; you would not let me correct you" (Jeremiah 2:30 GNB). Again He tried to call back His people with admonishments and chastenings until He had no other choice but to punish them in His holy wrath.

If God is Love, why does He punish mankind, His children, with manifestations of His wrath and severe judgments? For the very reason that He loves them. He cannot bear to see the world being turned into hell and filled with abominations that make people despair. Yes, if God did not intervene with judgment, He would be treating mankind cruelly, for then the hell-like conditions on earth would become permanent. And so He sends judgment upon this sin-laden earth, where hell is already manifesting itself. Through judgment He wants to deliver us from the hell-like conditions. He does not want us to become satanic ourselves. He intervenes and manifests His wrath, so that mankind cannot go on living in sin and vice. In the hour of judgment He will punish us in His holy wrath if previously we refused to humble ourselves beneath His chastening hand.

Though Saviour of mankind and the very essence of love, Jesus still had to pronounce a judgment upon Jerusalem: "The days shall come upon you, when your enemies will...dash you to the ground, you and your children within you, and they will not leave one stone upon another in you; because you did not know the time of your visitation" (Luke 19:43f.). And so when chastenings come into our lives, how vital it is that we understand:

"Now is the time of gracious visitation when the Lord is disciplining me and wants to bring about something wonderful in me. Now is the time when He has blessing, fruit and everlasting joy in store for me. But if I don't accept it, judgment will follow."

Everything depends on our taking the warnings of judgment seriously. Long ago His people did not want to take Jesus' warning of judgment seriously. Wasn't Jesus the Saviour, who did only good, as everyone saw? Yet He said that the city of Jerusalem would be levelled to the ground and destroyed "because you did not know the time of your visitation". The prophecy was then literally fulfilled, for every word pronounced by Jesus is Yea and Amen. He acts according to His word.

In those days people mocked at the prophecy, saying it would not come true, for years passed by without anything happening. But then came a day, the Friday before the Feast of the Passover, A.D. 70, the same day on which Jesus had been crucified. Suddenly the Roman army came into view. In three columns they advanced on the city, one of the columns encamping at roughly the same spot on the Mount of Olives where Jesus had prophesied that ramparts would be thrown up round the city. The judgment of God corresponded to what Jesus had once been made to suffer. A forest of crosses encircled the city, and hanging upon them were Jews crucified by the Romans.

We too shall come under the judgment and punishment of God if we have not submitted to His chastenings − for His words always come true. We cannot live on the forgiveness of Jesus in order to continue sinning — that is treating grace cheaply. Jesus said to the man healed at the Pool of Bethesda, "Sin no more, that nothing worse befall you" (John 5:14). After showing us grace, God waits for us to turn from our sinful ways and attitude, for otherwise we are threatened by judgment. But if we cannot bear to hear the word "judgment" and if we reject God as the Judge, we have already fallen under His judgment. For then we belong to the Pharisees, who did not want to heed Jesus' words, "For judgment I came into this world" (John 9:39). For all their piety they did not take God's judgment seriously. And so they came under judgment, as Jesus had warned them: "How are you to escape being sentenced to hell?" (Matthew 23:33). Even here on earth most of the Pharisees whom Jesus addressed were struck by the terrible judgment that descended upon Jerusalem — they and their children with them.

Just as judgment descended upon Jerusalem long ago and struck those who rejected the very thought of judgment, so will judgment befall us if instead of humbling ourselves beneath the mighty hand of God when He chastens us, we resist. Yes, according to Scripture judgment will then befall us: we shall be condemned along with the world. And the whole world is threatened by judgment. The earth and the works that are in it will be burned up (2 Peter 3:10b RAV).

Who will be destroyed during this judgment? The Apostle Peter writes that the earth has been "stored up for fire, being kept until the day of judgment and destruction of ungodly men" (2 Peter 3:7). In other words, the godless will come under judgment — those who did not want to know anything about God, those who did not want to submit to His will and chastenings, rebelling instead and saying No to His will. In so doing they led God-detached lives even if they may have thought themselves very devout. Fear and trembling should seize us at the words in the Revelation of John, "The great day of his wrath has come [a reference to the end times], and who is able to stand?" (Revelation 6:17 RAV). The vital question is: Will I be able to stand in this time? He who lets himself be chastened and judged and who passes through the refining fire of divine judgment beforehand will then be under the grace of the Lord.

We can sense how great the grace of God is in leading us along paths of chastening and discipline when we visualize the divine judgments of wrath hanging over our world. Holy Scripture indicates their proportions and frightfulness. In Isaiah, for instance, we read, "Behold, the day of the Lord comes, cruel, with wrath and fierce anger, to make the earth a desolation and to destroy its sinners from it" (Isaiah 13:9). In the following verse the prophet went on to say, and later Jesus would say virtually the same: "The stars of the heavens and their constellations will not give their light; the sun will be dark at its rising and the moon will not shed its light."

Many other passages in the Prophets refer to the terrible judgment. "I will punish the world for its evil, and the wicked for their iniquity...I will make the heavens tremble, and the earth will be shaken out of its place, at the wrath of the Lord of hosts in the day of his fierce anger" (Isaiah 13:11a,13); "Behold, the Lord will lay waste the earth [again, a statement confirmed by scientists today with regard to a coming nuclear war] and make it desolate, and he will twist its surface and scatter its inhabitants" (Isaiah 24:1); "The earth is utterly broken, the earth is rent asunder, the earth is violently shaken" (Isaiah 24:19); "Draw near, O nations, to hear, and hearken, O peoples! Let the earth listen, and all that fills it; the world, and all that comes from it. For the Lord is enraged against all the nations, and furious against all their host, he has doomed them, has given them over for slaughter...All the host of heaven shall rot away" (Isaiah 34:1ff.).

Each passage points to the same thing: the wrath of God will descend upon all nations; the whole world will be punished, laid waste and made desolate; and all because of man's wickedness and guilt. Yes, even the sun, moon and stars will have a part in expressing God's wrath. Though previously inconceivable, these events are now within the realm of possibility. This is proof that we have entered the apocalyptic age.

What is our attitude as we approach these judgments of wrath that threaten our world? Are we now taking every opportunity to be prepared by God along paths of chastening, so that we shall not be judged along with the world in the coming time of affliction? God, our heavenly Father, wants to carry us through in His arms and let us experience many miraculous instances of His protection. This is what He has in mind when He now chastens us. He intends to do us good afterwards – in the time of great affliction that lies ahead.

In the time of distress God will overwhelm us with goodness and we shall worship the Father for His immeasurable love, our hearts filled with amazement. How we shall thank Him for having chastened us previously in order to prepare us for such inexpressibly comforting tokens of His love and wonder-working power in the time of disaster! And one day above we shall scarcely be able to grasp the eternal joys that He has laid up for us. Rejoicing, we shall then join in the song of thanksgiving: "I thank You for having humbled and chastened me in order to bestow upon me goodness, joys and blessings in abundance. My Father, You are Love — nothing but Love!"

Yes, God chastens those whom He loves!

Three Tricks of Satan to Cripple Us Spiritually

Satan's lie is:
Chastenings make us unhappy. How can God be a God of Love if He chastens us?

The truth is:
The heavenly Father uses chastenings — provided we accept them — to bring us special blessings, good things, happiness and peace like a river.

Satan's lie is:
We don't need chastenings because of our sins. These sins don't matter. We have a right to live without suffering. And that is our aim.

The truth is:
Our faults and sins matter a great deal. They cause us much trouble even in this life, standing in the way of our happiness for time and eternity. Thus chastenings of God, which purge away sin, actually serve to our happiness and are the key to heaven.

Satan's lie is:
If I am converted, if I believe in Jesus, if I am baptized or even baptized in the Spirit, I have no more need of chastenings.

The truth is:
Faith in the victory of Jesus, in the blood of the Lamb, and in the working of the Holy Spirit, is not in itself sufficient to sanctify us. Chastenings are also necessary, for as it is written, God chastens us so that we shall partake of His holiness — suffering brings glory (cf. 2 Corinthians 4:17f.; Romans 8:17f.).

Therefore:
"Have you forgotten the exhortation which addresses you as sons? — 'My son, do not regard lightly the discipline of the Lord, nor lose courage when you are punished by him. For the Lord disciplines him whom he loves...' They [our earthly fathers] disciplined us for a short time at their pleasure, but he disciplines us for our good, that we

54

may share his holiness. For the moment all discipline seems painful rather than pleasant; later it yields the peaceful fruit of righteousness to those who have been trained by it" (taken from Hebrews 12).

Seven Tips on How to Be Happy in the Midst of Suffering

Give thanks in advance
on paths of suffering and chastening for the wonderful outcome that the Lord has prepared.

Live in expectation
of the wonderful gift and the abundance of good things the heavenly Father has in store for His child at the end of a path of chastening.

Humble yourself
beneath the mighty hand of God as it strikes you, and He will purge away more and more of the bad and sinful parts in you, which are the real source of your unhappiness.

Do not resist
chastening and suffering, for then you erect a barrier against God, preventing Him from filling your life with the good things that He wants to give you. Say, "Yes, Father", and His love and joy will flow into your heart.

Think good things of God
and trust that He has only the very best intentions even if His leadings seem incomprehensible to you — and you will experience His goodness amid suffering.

Trust the Father's love
in the assurance that He will never strike you too heavy a blow, and your trust will open wide His heart. You will become happy and receive many blessings on paths of suffering and chastening.

Think of eternity
and you will consider chastening an act of grace, since it keeps you from being tormented for ever in the kingdom of horrors, helping you instead to reach the heavenly goal of glory.

Saying Yes to our chastenings
is like turning a key
that unlocks the treasure chests
of divine blessing and goodness
hidden in chastenings.

Father,
I Thank You for Guiding My Way *

2. Father, I thank You in midst of my pain;
   Father, I thank You again and again.
   Chastening is the best "bread" for me;
   Chast'ning will end my sin's misery.

3. Father, Your goodness fills each of Your
       deeds;
   Father, Your chast'ning is what my soul needs.
   Father, the outcome of paths of pain
   Can be but blessing and glorious gain.

* Taken from M. Basilea Schlink, MY FATHER, I
  TRUST YOU, 38 Songs of Trust and Dedication.

4. Into Your hands I commit all, my Lord.
   For I know suff'ring will bring rich reward.
   I love the hand that is chast'ning me,
   For it is training and healing me.

5. Firm shall my hold of my Father's hand be;
   Safe through the darkest night you will lead
      me.
   Father, then bring me home to the throne,
   Through pain transform me and grant me a
      crown.

6. Never will You disappoint me, I know;
   Though great my sin, greater love still You
      show.
   I trust Your love in the darkest night;
   You've always brought Your child help and
      light.

7. Joy after suff'ring is always Your way;
   This I believe, I'm expecting today.
   Worship and honour to You I'll bring.
   When You chastise, songs of trust I'll sing.

8. You always love me, of this I am sure.
   This I proclaim whene'er Satan draws near.
   You always guide me with wisdom and care
   And never give me too much to bear.

9. At the right moment Your help always comes
   As You have promised and Your Word pro-
      claims.
   Father, Your chast'ning is love indeed;
   Goodness and mercy You show to me.

10. Almighty Father, majestic and great,
    Whom all the angels must serve and obey,
    You send them out to Your child in need,
    Showing Your might and assisting me.

11. So I'll endure in distress and dark night.
    Soon You will show me the bright morning
        light.
    Countless the times You've poured blessings
        on me.
    Father, my heart thanks You gratefully.

The way to joy —
joy here on earth and in heaven —
is paved with chastenings.
If you want your life
to end in the joy of heaven,
choose this way.

Prayer

Loving Father,

We thank You for going to so much trouble to bring us up. We worship You for the depths of Your love to us sinful beings — a love that has never tired of working in us although we have disappointed You a thousand times over — a love that has no rest until You have achieved the objective of Your paths of chastening: to transform us into the image of Your

Son and bring us to glory. For all eternity we shall thank You for not giving us up. Otherwise we would be lost for ever and abandoned to eternal judgment.

And so we humble ourselves before You and ask Your forgiveness for so often resisting You when You try to set us right in Your fatherly love. You have only good intentions for us. For each one of us You have a specific plan to bring us up the right way, so that we might experience release from the various sins that cling to us and separate us from You. Forgive us that we were often unwilling to submit to Your chastenings, which would have brought us release. And then we have even made You reproaches, although we have only ourselves to blame if we are unhappy! But now we want to renounce all grumbling and complaining, all thoughts of mistrust. We commit ourselves anew to You and give You our Yes to every chastening, trusting that Your ways are always right and that they will do us good, bringing us happiness and blessing for time and eternity. We praise Your fatherly will, which cannot but overwhelm us with goodness already here on earth at the end of paths of chastening.

May our loving act of dedication to Your chastenings bring You joy, beloved Father, when today You are deeply grieved by all those who rebel against Your will. With all our hearts we thank You for making us a special offer of grace as we approach the great end-time judgments: if we allow Your loving hand to correct and discipline us now, You will not have to condemn us along with the world when Your wrath descends upon the earth. And so we want to come before You now — each one of us — and say when we sense Your chastening hand upon us:

> Loving Father, I am Your child and I trust in Your love. So discipline and chasten me. Do with me as You please, if only You may achieve Your objective with me and find in my life the fruit of Your love.

Amen.

to one of today's most pertinent questions, "What comes after death?"

REPENTANCE –
THE JOY-FILLED LIFE 80pp.
Repentance – a golden key that opens the door to a joy-filled life. It has power to transform hearts and situations.

MY ALL FOR HIM 160pp.
"As I read this book, my heart yearned to love our Lord more. But it yearned most hopefully! For Mother Basilea does not merely express the depth of her own love for Jesus. She also shows how we too may ourselves experience it deeply. This book will warm the hearts of those who long to love our dear Lord more."

FATHER OF COMFORT
(Daily Readings) 128pp.
These brief daily devotions help us develop a personal relationship of love with God the Father. They are intended to nurture our trust and faith in Him.

HIDDEN IN HIS HANDS 96pp.
An encouraging selection of spiritual devotions. As we read this book, we shall discover how to experience security in God, and this will return to us as a source of strength and comfort in times of hardship.

THE CHRISTIAN'S VICTORY 192 pp.
Prescriptions of "spiritual medicine" for 45 differ-

ent sins. This intriguing book not only brings to light the sins which mar the Christian's life, but it also helps us to recognize them in our personal lives and points out the remedy.